BUY YOUR NEXT HOME

WITH CONFIDENCE

BY

Nadir S. Zulqernain, Ph.D.

This book gets into the nuts and bolts of a streamlined process for buying a home. It doesn't matter if you're a first-time homebuyer or a seasoned one, this book will help you immensely.

The home buying experience can create anxiety and uncertainty for many people. This occurs mainly due to unfamiliarity with the process, the sheer number of people involved and the amount of events that occur before you get to the end and your real estate broker hands you the keys to your new home.

This book takes the mystery out of home buying by laying things out in simple and easy to understand terms. The chapters follow the path preferred by all prudent homebuyers. By understanding and adopting the systems that have been explained in this book, you will be able to recognize and monitor each phase with the confidence that comes from being *in the know* – and remain in control throughout the home buying process.

Copyright © 2019 Growth By Design, Inc.

All Rights Reserved.

Published by Growth By Design, Inc. Bellevue, WA. The author can be reached through the publisher at nsz818@gmail.com

Disclaimer:

The U.S. Copyright Act of 1976 and all applicable international, federal, state and local laws protect this publication. All rights are reserved, including resale rights. You are not permitted to sell, reproduce, or transmit this book in part or in full, without first obtaining the express written permission of the publisher. To contact Growth By Design, Inc., please send an email to nsz818@gmail.com

This publication intends to provide authoritative and accurate information regarding the subject matter, based on personal experience and anecdotal evidence. The author and publisher have made every reasonable attempt to be correct. They make no representations or warranties concerning the completeness of the contents of this book and expressly disclaim any implied warranties of merchantability or fitness for a specific purpose. The publisher is not engaged in rendering legal, accounting, or other professional advice or services. If legal advice or additional expert assistance is required, retain the services of a competent professional person.

ISBN: 9781095699782

The first edition produced and printed in the United States of America in 2019.

DEDICATION

I dedicate this book to my clients. You have taught me a lot. I am forever grateful for your immense support.

ABOUT THE AUTHOR

Nadir S. Zulqernain, Ph.D., has been involved in the real estate business for more than twenty five years. His expertise comes from being engaged in various aspects of the real estate business. He owned numerous residential properties and commercial projects and has experience in rezoning and dealing with other aspects of land development.

He relished selling real estate in one of the largest waterfronts in the world, Kauai, Hawaii. He loves helping seasoned and first-time homebuyers and home sellers in the Greater Seattle Area of Washington State just as much.

For almost a decade, during this time, he also owned and operated a highly successful mortgage-banking firm. He gained invaluable understanding of home valuations and mortgage financing during that endeavor.

These treasured experiences have given him a unique understanding of the nuances involved in a home buying experience. He thoughtfully developed efficient and professional systems and processes to make it easy and fun for homebuyers acquire a home that meets their needs and desires for a price that makes sense, enabling them to stay in control.

You can learn more about the author's real estate business at brokernadir.com and about his coaching and mentoring business at mentorforhire.com

TESTIMONIALS

Zulqernain accomplishments have been recognized and applauded throughout his career.

Report on Business a magazine published by Canada's premier newspaper The Globe and Mail named him *"one of the fifty most influential persons."*

The Peak, Hong Kong called him *"an investment guru who mixes worldly-wise charisma with a sound business sense."*

Below is a glance into what his clients and peers have said about their real estate experience with him.

"You understood and were responsive to my needs. You get the highest marks in your knowledge of different aspects of purchase & sale, keeping me fully informed and especially of your negotiation skills. Having dealt with realtors in the past, I can say that you are truly a professional. Your passion for Real Estate is what I look for when hiring somebody. Everything you did exceeded my expectations. I will refer you to everyone that I know. They would be foolish to use anyone else."
Charles Borges de Oliveira – President

"Nadir is really well versed in helping brokers do what is best for clients."

JW Webb. President. Professional Realty Services.

"Nadir was in integral part in purchasing my first home! I initially consulted with Nadir on what steps I would need to take to position myself to purchase my first home. Not only did Nadir walk me through that process step by step, when I decided to proceed he continually advised and kept me informed throughout the whole process from beginning to end. I can't thank him enough for taking the extra time — it was the best home buying experience. His professionalism is stellar and I highly recommend him!"

Melissa Gray. A First Time Home Buyer.

TABLE OF CONTENTS

INTRODUCTION 11

CHAPTER ONE 16
HOMEBUYING BASICS

CHAPTER TWO 23
MONEY MATTERS

CHAPTER THREE 43
FINDING YOUR IDEAL HOME

CHAPTER FOUR 59
FIND THE PERFECT ONE

CHAPTER FIVE 80
OFFER TO MUTUAL ACCEPTANCE

CHAPTER SIX 100
FROM ACCEPTANCE TO CLOSE

CHAPTER SEVEN 130
IN CONCLUSION

INTRODUCTION

"Diligence is the mother of good luck."
Benjamin Franklin

Homebuyers must navigate three separate yet entwined paths prudently.

1) Cope with financial, legal, procedural and other related matters.
2) Find the right house in the desired neighborhood at the right price.
3) Stay in control throughout the process and comprehend who is involved and what function each person performs.

The information in this book will help you accomplish all of the above, with the confidence of those who have the inside knowledge.

This book is based on my personal practices as a real estate broker, and on experiences of those I have helped acquire homes and mortgage financing for more than twenty years. I work with both, the buyers and the sellers, and therefore have a thorough knowledge of both sides of a real estate transaction. I have also owned a mortgage company. This combined and acquired real estate knowledge and work experience further enhances my grasp of the home acquisition process.

I am blessed to have worked with many satisfied and repeat clients over the years. In this book, I spell out the path that those people followed to a fantastic home buying experiences.

The acquisition of a home is one of life's most significant undertakings. Deciding on what kind of a house to purchase, which neighborhood to live in, and what features in an ideal home to look for can prove to be challenging. *Your new home must meet your housing needs – and you must be able to afford it.*

The home buying process is by no means an easy one. Searching for your ideal home can be a daunting task.

One can liken the process of buying a home to putting together the pieces of a jigsaw puzzle. For optimum appreciation and satisfaction, the right pieces must come into the right places; otherwise, the overall effort goes to waste. Similarly, when buying a home, all the critical parts – location, features, agency, negotiation, finances, and several other items must come together in perfect alignment, and on time for the purchase to be successful and the home buyer to be fulfilled and satisfied.

It involves lots of paperwork, processes, inspections, deliberations, negotiations, legalities and technicalities and of course, *finances*.

The information in this book will familiarize you with each aspect of the home buying process. It will also help you attain a level of confidence that comes only from being *in the know*.

The information in this book is intended to benefit two groups of people.

The first group is homebuyers. This book carries valuable information for those who are considering the purchase of a home, either now or in the near future. If you fall into this category, this book will do you a world of good, save you from a great deal of aggravation and stress and may also save you several thousands of dollars.

You will learn all that you need to know about home buying; how to find a home that meets your needs and desires, how to make a winning offer, how to negotiate successfully, how to easily wade your way through a mound of paperwork, and many other valuable tips.

If you have never bought a home before and are on the verge of making your first purchase, you cannot do so without the principles outlined in this book.

The other group of people who will find the information in this book to be valuable is the real estate professionals. By learning and imbibing the principles shared in this book, you will become equipped to serve your clients better and thus grow your business more rapidly.

In any business enterprise, serving your customer as best as possible is essential. Due to the significant and long-lasting impact of a home buying experience on our customers, this aspect is even more critical in the business of selling real estate.

In writing his book, I have drawn from the expertise gained through more than two decades of hands-on experience in dealing with different aspects of home buying and selling experience and other real estate aspects, in different geographical locations, at different levels, and from different perspectives.

Read this book with an open mind. Be willing to unlearn, relearn and learn, all for the sake of smooth, hassle-free and successful home buying experiences.

Happy reading and happy home hunting!

CHAPTER ONE

HOMEBUYING BASICS

A home is still the biggest asset that most Americans own.

Mark Zandi

The home buying process can be complicated. This is because several different service providers and their unique set of rules, guidelines, and protocol have to merge seamlessly so that you can acquire your home.

Real Estate brokers, mortgage lenders, licensed home inspectors, licensed appraisers, and closing agents and attorneys – each must work independently and adhere to their industry-specific rules while supporting and complementing each other's work in order to serve the best interest of the client – you, the homebuyer.

The process of finding a home that meets your needs and desires can be a daunting one. The best solution is to hire a seasoned, competent real estate professional and let him do all the legwork. It is critical that you engage a broker who takes the time to understand your needs and desires – and possesses the know-how, the tools, the skill-set, and resources to deliver the best possible results for you.

This is the best way to acquire a home that meets your needs and desires, is located in the neighborhood that you desire – and its price makes sense.

We will discuss the home buying process from each angle and help you better understand the role of each of the parties involved.

Financing, legal and procedural considerations must be at the top of a relatively long list of critical matters to be considered by homebuyers. This is true for the first-time homebuyers and for the folks who may have bought and sold homes or are now selling theirs to buy another one.

Navigate three separate paths

In the introduction I wrote that homebuyers must navigate three separate yet integrated paths prudently.

1. Coping with financial, legal, procedural and other related matters.
2. Being able to find the right house in the desired neighborhood at the right price.
3. Staying in control throughout the process and comprehend who is involved and what function each person performs.

The information in this book will provide you with insights so that you can accomplish all of the above.

First-time homebuyers face a unique set of challenges when they start the process of acquiring a home. They have never gone through an experience like this so it can be overwhelming. Finding the right home in the right neighborhood; one that is within your budget, can become a daunting task.

Let us discuss coping with financial, legal, procedural and other related matters. To understand this aspect better, let us break down the financial considerations into two categories, *internal* and *external.*

Internal refers to your personal financial matters. It denotes our financial ability and emotional capacity to undertake what maybe the largest financial investment you would ever make.

Purchasing a home is a major financial undertaking. You must do your calculations carefully, use accurate numbers and have realistic expectations.

Altering a house purchase is costly

You will need to restructure your financing to modify the terms of your mortgage loan, also know as *refinancing your mortgage* – doing so can be costly. The only way to get out of it altogether is to sell the house. The cost of selling a home varies from State to State, and is usually between six to ten percent. You will need to have owned your home for at least three to five years, sometimes even longer before you can recoup that cost. It is imperative that you calculate your numbers carefully and accurately.

Are you a prudent homebuyer?

You must figure out your finances before you enter into a contract. You must be realistic and precise about those numbers. Your budget must take into account every item, including allocation for contingencies. You also need to factor in unexpected repairs after you move in, and aesthetic improvements to the property that most people want to make after they move into a new home.

Protect yourself against financial hardships, emotional stress, and lost opportunities by having an open and honest conversation about your internal financial considerations. Going through this phase will also prepare and equip you to handle your external financial matters more favorably.

External financial considerations refer to your ability to organize your financial affairs, documentation, and creditworthiness so that you can obtain the mortgage financing for your purchase and satisfy various other financial demands.

After sorting out your internal financial matters, your next step must be to figure out the specifics of the financing of your intended acquisition. A small number of homebuyers pay cash for their purchase. Most people need a mortgage loan to buy a house.

Mortgage lenders take two elements into consideration when evaluating a loan application.

a) The borrower
b) The property

The borrower pays the lender back and the property is the lender's collateral if the borrower is unable to repay the loan. We will discuss this aspect in detail in the next chapter.

CHAPTER TWO

MONEY MATTERS

All homeowners in America may deduct mortgage interest on their first and second homes.
Mathew Desmond

In this chapter, we will discuss how to go about shopping, applying and obtaining financing for your intended home purchase.

Creditworthiness is a combination of three things.

1. Documenting the source of your income.
2. Track record of repaying your previous debts.
3. Documenting the source of the funds that you intend to use for your down payment.

Mortgage lenders must adhere to an extensive and rigid set of rules and guidelines when making loans. The discussion that follows will give you the right know-how so you can be well equipped to get your loan application approved.

It is crucial to understand the nuances of this phase and avoid challenges and delays when it is time to close your transaction. It is not uncommon for a transaction to fall through at the last minute because of certain technicalities that could have been easily avoided by being adequately prepared.

There is a massive amount of specific lending rules and guidelines that all parties involved must follow. The information herein will not make you an expert in these technicalities. You will, however, be able to have a meaningful conversation with your mortgage loan representative and ask the right questions that the former is supposed to answer with pertinent hard and fast details and facts.

Documenting the source of your income

Lenders are required to verify two years of your income history to establish income that will be eligible to be used in their calculations. In order to do this, they will require you to produce the following documents:

1) Your W2 forms for the most recent two years.
2) Your two most recent paystubs.

If you are self-employed, you will be asked to produce your two most recent tax returns with all of its schedules. The average of the last two years of your income will be marked as your eligible income. It is to be noted that self-employed people will to have to jump through a few additional hoops.

Another thing to be noted is that you must have earned your income from in the same line of business during the most recent two years. Changing employers will not create an issue. However, changing your line of work will affect you adversely.

If you were a full-time employee and decided to go into business for yourself, you will need to have been in business for a minimum of two years for your income to be eligible – even if the line of work had remained the same as when you were an employee.

If you have gaps in your employment history over the two most recent years, you will be required to provide a satisfactory explanation for those gaps. The gist of that explanation will determine your eligibility.

In all, you need to have at least two years of steady income, in the same line of work and you must be able to document the source of that income.

Track record of repaying previous debts

Mortgage lenders want to have a complete picture of your history of repaying debts. They do this by obtaining your credit reports from each of the three major credit bureaus.

The credit report that the mortgage lenders use is called a tri-merge report, also known as Residential Mortgage Credit Report (RMCR). This report is a single, easy-to-read (for a mortgage lender, not so much for the consumers) complete report that is compiled from the individual credit reports issued by the three major consumer credit bureaus.

This report often differs from the single bureau *Free Credit Report* that consumers get, because those reports do not include the information from the other two credit bureaus. A word of caution here – think twice before submitting your information on those *check your credit score for free* Apps. Doing so can expose you to all sorts of problems, the worst being, identity theft.

TV commercials and incomplete information found on the internet have perpetuated the myth that your credit score is one magic number that you can move up quickly – his information is profoundly misleading. The process that a lender uses to calculate the credit score that will form the basis of their loan offer to you, which in turn will establish the interest rate and loan fees of your mortgage, is more complex than that.

Your credit scores, obtained through RMCR are the basis of the loan terms that you will receive.

Lenders base their decision on your middle credit score. For couples, the lower of the two credit scores will establish the grid to be used.

For example, let's say Judy and Mark apply for a loan. When the lender looks at the RMCR, Judy's credit scores turn out to be 637, 661 and 708. Judy's lender will use 661. Mark's scores turn out to be 649, 683 and 731. The lender will use 683 for Mark. Applying the rule of lower of the two middle scores as described above to this example, 661 will determine the terms of the loan.

Lenders establish ranges or bands of credit scores. Whichever group your credit score falls into, will determine the interest rate of your mortgage loan. These bands can vary from lender to lender; however, they tend to run from 620 to 660, from 661 to 700, from 700 to 740 and above 740.

The interest rate of your loan will depend upon the group of your credit score. In the example given above, even though Mark's middle score is 683, which falls in the 680 to 720 range. Judy's score of 661 will be used as the basis of the loan offer. The interest rate, and in some situations, even the loan fees will be higher for 661 than they would have been for 683.

Credit scores are based on complex algorithms that take a myriad of financial activities into account. Negative activity affects them more quickly because the even that caused it has already occurred. Positive activity must get seasoned before having an impact and reflect an improvement in the score.

There are a limited type of credit accounts that can show a quick improvement, and thus an improved credit score. However, this will vary for each person and on the type of account. The best person to assist you in this regard will be the mortgage lender that you choose to work with.

For the reasons outlined above, I recommend to my clients that the first step in their home buying process must be getting *an underwriter's loan approval.*

It will save you time, money and aggravation to get a complete understanding of your financial options earlier on in the process. You will have time to improve your credit scores if it is necessary. It will also help you pin down exactly what you can afford, which in turn will make your home search a lot easier.

Pre-Approval is better than pre-qualification

After establishing your *internal financial* matters and have an in-depth understanding of what you will need to handle the *external financial* issues let us discuss how that aspect will work.

Exactly how much money are you eligible to borrow and what conditions will you have to meet to get those funds? Only a lender can answer this question. You start the process of obtaining this answer by approaching a mortgage lender or broker directly.

I recommend that you first find and establish a relationship with a real estate professional that best suits your needs. Choosing the right real estate broker is paramount – I will discuss in detail exactly *how* you can find one, a little later, in this book.

Real estate brokers sift through and distinguish mortgage lenders who offer more favorable loan terms and better service to their clients. If you choose a real estate professional based on the criteria elaborated in the next chapter, you can take comfort in knowing that you will get the right advice from them. The real estate professional you choose should be able to ensure that the loan-qualifying phase goes smoothly.

Prequalifying for a mortgage loan is pretty easy. Yet, It's practically purposeless. Having a pre-qualification letter just indicates that you discussed your financial situation with someone at the mortgage lenders office. It's understood that you neither provided any documentation nor did the lender verify any of the verbal information that you provided.

The lender merely considered the broader guidelines and concluded that you are likely to be approved for a loan of up to a certain amount; then issued you a letter stating that they have pre-qualified your loan application.

Most pre-qualification letters include paragraphs starting with *"this is subject to"* followed by a list of several items that they would need before an approval can be issued.

Note that the homebuyers, and real estate professionals who rely on such letters, often get their offers rejected. When I see pre-qualification letters like this while representing a seller, I recommend to my client that they decline the offer. It's because this letter does not indicate that the buyer has the funds to complete the transaction.

If your offer to purchase a home is to carry any weight, it must include an *underwritten pre-approval letter*. For you to obtain such a letter, you will need to submit all of the documents that we discussed in the previous section. The lender will then verify the information on those documents. Some of the verifications are done verbally, others in writing. After the verification process is complete, the lender will do an initial underwriting.

Most lenders use automated underwriting systems for loan approval. They submit your loan application through the underwriting system; which will reject or approve the loan application and produce either a list or reasons for rejection or a list of approval conditions.

Because it is at such an early stage, even a rejection, accompanied by the reasons for loan being rejected is very helpful. Your loan officer can go through the specifics with you and make recommendations. There will be a list of conditions attached to the approval, which will spell out precisely what you need to provide for the loan to be finalized. Apparent reasons are present to vouch for the letter.

Because circumstance can change, lenders never issue a complete and final approval. A fundamental or material change in your situation can disqualify you for the loan, even though it was approved earlier. For instance, you could lose your job a week before the closing of the house – such a material fact will prevent the lender from advancing you the funds.

Lenders always check your credit just before the closing. It is imperative that you do not undertake any out of the norm expenses between the time that your loan application was initially approved until all of the paperwork is complete and the transaction has closed. If you are planning to make any big purchases, its best to put that off until after the house is actually yours.

The nightmare scenario that can develop if you have any last-minute issues with the financing of your new home is never pretty and is often very costly.

I cannot overstate the importance of getting a solid, fully underwritten loan approval before you start the process of buying a house. Make sure that you fully understand all of the loan conditions and stay within those guidelines.

Earnest Money and the Down Payment

Down Payment is the total amount of money that you contribute to the purchase price of the house. The rest comes from your mortgage loan.

Earnest money is a good faith deposit that accompanies your *written offer* to purchase the house. There are no hard and fast rules about how much, in dollars or percentage, does it need to be. It can vary from one or two percent to as much as ten percent or more.

The market conditions determine the amount, to some extent. If there are many more buyers than there are sellers, and bidding wars are going on, the higher earnest money deposits become a factor. If the reverse is true, then the sellers become more accommodating.

Rules about what happens to the earnest money deposit if the sale falls through vary from State to State. If the seller fails to perform, the funds would be returned to the buyer. However, if the buyer fails to complete the purchase contract, they may lose all or part of the earnest money deposit. Most States treat it as liquidated damages and have a preset limit to which a seller can be entitled. Having a detailed discussion about the rules that govern your earnest money deposit with your real estate broker, and to fully understand your options is vital.

Some key points to remember are:

a) Purchase and Sale contract dictates all aspects of the agreement. Read it. Make sure you understand how your earnest money deposit will be handled, in case you default. Ask these questions from your broker and make sure you are satisfied with the answers you get.

b) Insist on making the check payable to the closing agent and not to anyone else.

c) Ask your broker to explain to you how the earnest money deposit rules work in your State.

d) Get a receipt of your earnest money deposit, directly from the closing agent.

As a practical matter, earnest money disputes rarely occur. Washington State has streamlined rules and guideline for receiving, holding and the disposition of earnest money deposits. Our approved Purchase and Sale Agreement is written in a way to minimize this issue.

The disposition of earnest money deposit is also tied in with the contingencies written into the purchase and sale agreement. A seasoned real estate broker can help you navigate through this critical phase.

Earnest money deposit is part of your total down payment. It will be a *credit to the buyer* in the *final closing statement* that you will receive at closing.

Down Payment Funds

Several rules and guideline must be complied with when dealing with the down payment funds.

Sellers want to know if a buyer can come up with the money to complete the transaction. Federal and State regulators want to make sure that no money laundering or other illicit activities take place under the guise of a real estate transaction.

Mortgage lenders want to make sure that they advance funds to the right person and receive the correct collateral.

Each of these things is accomplished through various sets of rules and guidelines, which also serve to protect the buyer. Your broker and your *escrow closer* are two sources that will inform you of these specifics.

Proof of funds:

Buyers either pay the purchase price either with their funds or pay by a mortgage loan.

When a seller receives an offer to purchase from a buyer that is getting a mortgage loan to pay for that purchase, its is usually accompanied by a letter from a lender who has either pre-qualified or pre-approved the buyer. I discussed the distinction between these two types of letters in a previous section.

This letter from a lender helps the seller make an informed decision. A pre-approval letter assures the seller that the funds to close the transactions are present.

When the offer to purchase is on a cash basis, sellers usually require proof that the buyer has the money to complete the transaction, or *proof of funds*. Bank statements from the buyer's accounts where the funds are deposited is considered a reliable *proof of funds*.

Sourcing and seasoning of funds:

When borrowing to buy a home, lenders require you to demonstrate the source of your down payment funds. Lenders do not like money that appears out of thin air into your account.

Sourcing refers to the requirement that you show the source of funds you intend to use for your down payment. However, this requirement kicks in only if the funds have been in your bank account for less than sixty days. You are not required to show the source of funds that you have had for more than sixty days. This is what is, meant by *seasoning*.

Your regular stream of income can easily be identified in your bank statements and is supported by the paystubs you provide to your lender. If an amount other than your regular deposits shows up within sixty days from closing, you will be required to show proof of how you came to have those funds.

Gift Funds:

Certain types of loans permit the borrower to use funds they receive as a gift from family members. These are called *gift funds*. Specific guidelines for that particular loan will determine how much of your down payment can include gift funds and how you may receive those funds. There are specific requirements for correctly documenting these gift funds. Often, it requires extra time.

It makes things more comfortable and stress-free when you give yourself ample time to get organized and adequately prepare sufficiently for the acquisition of your dream home. *Get yourself a seasoned pro and start early.*

CHAPTER THREE

FINDING YOUR IDEAL HOME

To be an ideal guest, stay at home.
E. W. Howe

What is an ideal home? Each of us has a different way to think about our *perfect home*. People place importance on different features of a home and its conveniences because they have varying priorities.

Now that you have gone through the loan approving process described in an earlier chapter, you have learned how to obtain a loan that fits your circumstances. You have also looked at your available finances and have established a firm dollar amount as the top price that you will pay for your new home. Thence, we will proceed further.

Important tip #1:

Give yourself a ten percent discount before you start your home search. Let us say that your loan approval is for a purchase price of five hundred thousand dollars and you intended to make a down payment of ten percent. Your finances are in great shape to acquire a house for that price. *Drop that target price to four hundred and fifty thousand dollars – and do not tell anyone about it.* Make it your secret. Refrain from sharing this information with your lender and your real estate broker.

Any number of circumstances could develop when this extra cushion comes very handy.

If you follow this advice, some day after you have purchased your home, you will be compelled to seek me out and drop me a *thank you* note.

Make a list:

Start your home search by preparing a comprehensive list that has two categories. The longer and more detailed the list, the more beneficial it will be for you. The more effort and thought you put into making this list, the smoother, and more productive, your home search will be. Avoid rushing and hasting. Be thorough and detailed.

You will avoid a great deal of aggravation and perhaps save thousands of dollars by making this list and then using it, as I am about to describe it. This list will equip you with the right tools and the mindset of a *prudent homebuyer*. You will easily recognize the house that will meet most of your requirements, and you will be able to acquire it at a price that will make sense.

Make *essentials* the first category of the list. Under this category, itemize each feature you must have in your new home. Make *desirables* the second category. Here, enumerate what you wish to have in your home.

For example, if your minimum requirement is three bedrooms but having a fourth one will be nice, then, three bedrooms will go in the *essentials* category, and the fourth will be in the *desirables* category. If you want a home office, yet can live without one that will go in the *desirables* category.

The next step is to attach a value, between one and five, to each item in each of the two categories. Five is to be the highest, and one is to be the lowest. This part of the process can take time and be a lot of fun.

Keep this list handy when you start looking at homes. Use it to check off various items and total up the scores. Most of my clients enter the homes they see into an Excel or a Google sheet and use the scoring system to identify their preferences – and narrow down their choices.

I have walked through hundreds, if not thousands of homes, mostly with people who were considering buying that home. The fact is that no home turns out to be *perfect* for anyone. I have had clients who build a house from scratch. They may have spent months designing it and many more months, building it. Soon after they moved in, they discovered some little variance that they would have liked to have. That is human nature. This phenomenon holds particularly true when families are involved.

Grab your list and start searching.

Select the neighborhood you want to live in:

You are almost ready to get in the car and start looking at houses in person. It is not only the house that must meet your needs and desires – it must be located in the right neighborhood as well.

Technology has made house hunting a lot easier than it used to be. That goes for neighborhoods as well, now better known as *communities*. Being old fashioned I prefer *neighborhoods*.

Start with a Google map search. You can assess a great deal by just looking at a location and its surroundings on a map. Then work your way through to websites that will give you extensive information about the communities in that desired area. Use one or more websites to research the following:

- Housing data
- Livability scores
- Cost of living
- Amenities
- Crime rate
- Education

- Transportation
- Employment opportunities
- Median rents and home prices
- Percentage of rentals & owner occupied homes
- Weather

After finishing the online research, it is time to do some fieldwork. Go and spend several hours in your selected top two or three neighborhoods. Stop by at the local grocery store, the local park, and a local café. Engage in casual conversations with some folks living there. Ask them about the neighborhood and what they like or dislike about it. There is nothing better than hearing from the people who live there. This exercise will give you a sense of the place and first hand information on which to base your decision.

Save all the information that you gathered from these searches and your field trip, and have it at hand when you start to look at houses.

Start your search:

I have heard some pretty interesting stories about how people found their ideal home.

One of the top three of my most favorite homes that I lived in was in the Cherry Creek neighborhood on Downing Street in Denver, Co. It was a small house surrounded by huge mansion-like houses. I drove by it often and was awed by the enormous trees in its backyard. I grew to like it so much that I tracked down the owner and eventually purchased it. That was about twenty-five years ago. Times have changed now, and there are significantly simpler ways to find a home.

So, now, you have already decided upon and researched your desired neighborhood. By having made the list, you know precisely the kind of house you want to acquire. You also have a clear idea about the concessions you might have make, as far as your *essentials* and *desirables* are concerned.

Almost all the home searches start on the internet nowadays. There is a plethora of real estate related websites that you can go to and search for homes that are available for sale.

These websites fall into two main categories. Some sites are owned and operated by the real estate brokers and firms, like Re/Max, Keller Williams, Redfin, to name a few. These sites provide you information about homes that are on the market and the company whose site it is, hopes to capture your business. I have a site like that and would love for you to check it out at BrokerNadir.com. You may find it refreshingly different.

The other category is real estate advertising sites, like Craigslist, Facebook Marketplace, and Zillow. These sites are in the advertising business and use real estate properties as their niche to generate traffic and thus their revenue. Home sellers can advertise for free on these sites and homebuyers can check out what is available.

No set of rules and regulations related to real estate transactions govern any of these websites. There is no protection for the consumers.

Zillow is the most recognized name, and arguably, the number one site that people go to when searching for homes to rent or buy. One of Zillow's primary revenue source is the sale of leads to real estate professionals. When you search for homes on Zillow, your data is collected and sold at pretty hefty prices. Zillow is notorious for having highly inaccurate value estimates that are displayed next to the homes that you see on their website.

Some other websites operate on similar business models, but most of those are not widely known.

You can register and search on several sites at the same time. Regardless of the website you choose to initiate the search, you must keep the home search process separate from evaluating the real estate broker you will hire. We will get into the nitty-gritty of that subject in the next chapter.

Browse some of the websites that I have mentioned above and formulate an overview of what is available within your price range and in your preferred neighborhood.

What is an MLS and how does it work?

Multiple listing services, better known as MLS are private databases that either directly or indirectly, are owned by real estate professionals. There are some exceptions – in some cases, Counties or Real Estate Boards own the local MLS.

An MLS is usually organized at the County level. If a county is too small, then an MLS may cover more than one county. Each MLS has a unique name. For example, MLS that I belong to is called the Northwest Multiple Listing Service or NWMLS.

Licensed real estate professionals are not required to become a member of an MLS. However, given that more than ninety percent of real estate transactions involve a property listed on the local MLS, it is practically impossible to conduct any business without belonging to one.

MLS serves as the primary marketplace for residential real estate connecting buyers and sellers of homes, throughout the United States. This service saves everyone involved in a real estate transaction – buyers, sellers, and brokers – time and legwork in sorting through the properties on the market.

MLS provides these two most critical functions.

1. It delivers verified and accurate information about homes that are on the market. Real estate brokers can expose the property that they have been contracted to sell to thousands of potential buyers they would otherwise never reach. On the other hand, buyers can enjoy the benefit of instant access to listings that match their specified criteria.
2. It requires that all real estate brokers transparently publish and the commissions being paid on every transaction. MLS also requires them to spells out how those commissions will be shared between listing firms and selling firms. I will discuss how commissions work in the next chapter.

MLS is not a regulating body. That job rests with the Real Estate Commission in Washington State. A similar organization called The Real Estate Board may perform the function of establishing licensing rules in other States. The primary role of MLS is to manage the data and develop guidelines and best practices for the broker's cooperation with each other. This aspect ensures the fair and equal treatment of consumers.

All of the websites that I identified earlier; each one of them gets their data from their local MLS. That particular MLS has a say in how these websites utilize that data.

In recent years, technology has disrupted and modified many industries. The real estate industry is not an exception. A lot more information is readily and easily available to consumers through the internet.

MLS model has been around for almost one hundred years. It has evolved and kept up with the changing trends. It is a gross misconception that merely because information is readily available to everyone, consumers can conclude a real estate transaction directly, without the assistance of real estate professionals or real estate attorneys.

The most effective way to search for a home

The best way to search for your new home is to get the information, directly from your local MLS.

You browsed through various real estate website in the initial phase. Now, it is time to go to the source and get all of the facts about every home you wish to consider and evaluate. The professional real estate broker that you are now ready to hire has all that information and it is yours just by asking.

My local MLS has an awesome App that gives the user direct access to every single listing on the market. It provides all the data you need to make an informed decision. It has a built-in chat feature that makes it a breeze for my clients to ask me questions about any home that might interest them. It also enables all the members of the family to stay fully informed without the need for a chain of emails going back and forth. My clients love it. There is a direct link to it on brokernadir.com

You are ready to search for your new home. What you need now is a real estate broker who will help you find, research and evaluate the home you decide upon. She or he will also negotiate on your behalf. In the next chapter, I will go into more detail about how to select your real estate broker.

Real estate brokers belong to their local MLS. They have instant access to every single listing that comes on the market. They also have access to all of the background information about every listing, including any disclosure and other supporting documents.

When my clients choose to use the App that I mentioned above, they get instant access to all of that information as well.

A seasoned broker who is committed to serving his clients may also have access to properties that are not on the market yet. Those are called off-market properties. They may even know about sellers that are in the early stages of preparing their home to list. This type of access has apparent benefits. If you are an adventurous homebuyer, your broker can get you a list of potential or current *foreclosures, short sales and auctions*. The process of buying these homes is different, as are the financial requirements for that type of acquisition. Your broker can guide you through that.

There is a significant difference between data and information. Data are mostly tiny bits and pieces of information, just facts or figures. When data are processed, interpreted, organized, and structured to make them meaningful to a level where they can provide context, then it becomes information that you can utilize.

Most seasoned brokers have systems and networks that they use to harvest information about properties and neighborhoods. This valuable information cannot be found anywhere else.

That is what a top-notch real estate broker can do for you. They can help you organize the data you have gathered from your initial research and combine it with the data available for homes that are on the market. You can then make informed decisions that best serve your needs and desires.

CHAPTER FOUR

FIND THE PERFECT ONE

There was no big break, just years and years of work.

Paula Del Nunzio

Let us start this chapter with a question that more and more people ask these days. Do I really need a broker when buying a home? It is an important question. Especially since we live in an era where more and more industries have been disrupted by eliminating the middleman, so to speak.

To answer this question meaningfully, let's do a deep dive into how the real estate industry works. Thus you will better understand the agent or broker's role; their qualifications, their obligations, and their licensing requirements – and what a pivotal role they play in every transaction.

Let me introduce you to this *not-so-rare* a person found throughout this vast land of ours. There are many, and they are everywhere. In some parts of the country, she is known as an *agent*, and in other regions, he is known as a *broker*. Some other folks know her as a *realtor*.

We will discuss how these people become agents, brokers or realtors and what do these labels mean. We will also learn how to find a real estate professional that is just right for your circumstances and your needs, and most importantly, can help you acquire the home of your dreams for a price that will make sense.

You can then decide if you need to hire a professional to look after and protect your interests. In fact, the question then becomes what will ever keep you from hiring a top-notch professional who doesn't cost you a dime? Will you ever go to court without proper representation, especially if the other side said, *we will pay for it, and you can hire anyone you choose*?

How is the industry structured?

Understanding how the entire ecosystem of the real estate industry operates, you will gain practical inside information – and be able to function in this environment with confidence, protect your interests and acquire your new home without any hassles.

People who become real estate brokers come from diverse backgrounds, with varying interests and education level. Most people start in this business on a part-time basis and hold a second job while working with clients. The industry has a high turnover rate of brokers. The initial license is good for two years. Unfortunately, a high percentage of agents do not renew their licenses.

Licensing requirements vary from State to State. Each State has a set of rule or laws that govern the real estate licensing procedures, and define the relationship between consumers and licensees. A body, known as a *real estate commission or board* enforces these rules and regulations. The State Governor usually appoints members to this body.

These laws are designed to accomplish two things:

1. Define the role of real estate brokers and establish best business practices and ascertain professional standards.
2. Protect consumers from unsavory practices and facilitate a protected environment for real estate transactions.

In addition to these rules, the local MLS performs several important functions. While they do not play a role in licensing, they have their own guidelines and protocol that must be followed by their members. A real estate broker can hardly function without belonging to her local MLS, because that is where all the homes are listed.

There are multi-layered consumer protections in place. However, there is no substitute for consumers being fully informed and maintaining complete control over the home buying process.

National Association of Realtors (NAR) is the largest association in the real estate industry; it owns the trademark, *Realtor*. Real Estate agents who belong to this association are permitted to use the term '*Realtor*' on their business card to demonstrate their affiliation with that association.

NAR has an *all or nothing* policy. They require that everyone in a specific real estate office must join. Individual brokers do not get a choice to opt out. If a company has more than one office, some of these offices may belong to NAR and have *realtors* and other offices may not. The reverse is true as well. There are entire offices and companies that do not belong to the association. If an individual broker from one of those offices wants to join the association, she cannot. Whether or not one belongs to NAR is dictated by whether or not the office they are affiliated with belongs to NAR.

I am not a *Realtor*. In my opinion, belonging to the NAR might present some benefits for me personally; it does little to add value to my clients. My focus has always been on my clients.

I believe that the real estate industry is not only the backbone of our economy; it is also the purest form of capitalism. Real estate companies are as unique as the brokers who own and staff them. There are large, national firms and at the other spectrum, there are single operators, offering the exact same services. When you perceive *all real estate is local,* you will quickly understand that the variety makes choosing the right one, slightly tricky.

How does real Estate licensing work?

There are three tiers of real estate licensing in most States, although different States may have different terminologies. The first tier is a broker's license. In some States, brokers are referred to as *agents* – a term that was eliminated in Washington State, some time back. This license permits the holder to act as a real estate broker. It is illegal to engage in real estate brokerage types of activities unless of course, it is for your property.

The second tier of real estate license is that of a *managing broker*. This designation requires more experience, more training, and another written exam. Managing brokers carry a higher responsibility and are eligible to supervise other brokers in a specific office. A Managing Broker with a special endorsement is called a *designated broker*, which indicates an even higher level of supervisory role. A *designated broker* can oversee an entire Firm and all of its offices.

Most states do not require a person to have a college degree to be eligible to apply for any of the three tiers of licensing mentioned above. Applicants must take a ninety-hour course and take a test in a dedicated test facility. Licensing must be renewed every two years by taking a thirty-clock hour course. For the first renewal one needs to complete a ninety-clock hours course.

Responsibilities of a broker to his clients

Washington State has categorically defined seven key responsibilities and obligations that a broker owes to his or her clients. Other states have similar laws. You can obtain the specific list from your State's Department of Licensing.

Here is a slightly modified list of those obligations:

(a) To exercise reasonable skill and care;

(b) To deal honestly and in good faith;

(c) To present all written offers, written notices and other written communications to and from either party in a timely manner, regardless of whether the property is subject to an existing contract for sale or the buyer is already a party to an existing contract to purchase;

(d) To disclose all existing material facts known by the broker and not apparent or readily ascertainable to a party; provided that this subsection shall not be construed to imply any duty to investigate matters that the broker has not agreed to investigate;

(e) To account in a timely manner for all money and property received from or on behalf of either party;

(f) To provide a pamphlet on the law of real estate agency to all parties to whom the broker renders real estate brokerage services, before the party signs an agency agreement with the broker, signs an offer in a real estate transaction handled by the broker, consents to dual agency, or waives any rights, under (four other regulations, which I have not specified here) whichever occurs earliest; and

(g) To disclose in writing to all parties to whom the broker renders real estate brokerage services, before the party signs an offer in a real estate transaction handled by the broker, whether the broker represents the buyer, the seller, both parties, or neither party.

Brokers are also *required* to deliver a copy of the pamphlet on the *law of real estate agency*.

It is clear that the State regulators have taken significant steps to protect the consumer. Yet, it is of paramount importance that you, the consumer be diligent and cautious. By being knowledgeable about the industry and its inner workings, you will be able to protect yourself against even the unintended negligent conduct of an incompetent broker.

This burden of *being responsible for your actions* has also been placed on homebuyers by an underlying principal of real estate law, known as *Caveat Emptor;* Latin for *let the buyer beware.*

This principal holds that the buyer of a property has the burden of exercising proper care when purchasing real property. It is the buyer's responsibility to conduct the appropriate research and exercise caution when acquiring a property, and to make every reasonable effort to uncover any issues with it.

How do you recognize a *good broker?*

You recognize a good real estate broker the same way that you spot a good lawyer, a good doctor, a good dentist, or even a good gardener, house cleaner, or a contractor. You start by making sure that they are properly licensed, adequately trained and qualified to do what you may want to hire them to do.

As is the case with other professions, the real estate profession has its share of incompetent individuals. This problem is somewhat compounded due to a high percentage of people who either work on a part-time basis or do not make an effort to become proficient in various aspects of our profession.

In case of a real estate broker, for starters, you can log in to the Department of Licensing's website and look up their record. You want to make sure that they do not have any outstanding complaints against them, and have not been disciplined for incidents of inappropriate professional conduct.

There is some value to researching a particular broker online, however, by and large that does not produce quantifiable and reliable results. I know many top-notch brokers who have chosen not to have a significant online presence.

A subjective answer to the question is that a good broker is one who is duly licensed, has a robust knowledge base not only in the real estate business but also about the specific neighborhood where you wish to purchase your home. He must also be fully informed of the process of different types of real estate transactions and knowledgeable about the peripheral services and personnel that becomes a part of the transaction.

There are ancillary courses and training available. You might see some letters of the alphabet after an individual broker's name on his business cards. I must admit regrettably, that as a consumer, you cannot put much stock in that. As an example, CNE stands for Certified Negotiation Expert. Well, I could have taken that course for a couple of hundred bucks, either for a few hours in a classroom or online. I doubt that one can develop expertise in a complex subject such as *contract negotiations* in a few hours.

Remember, the most important thing is that you find a broker who is going to best serve your needs. You are the ideal person to make that determination. Next section covers this topic in detail.

How to find the one just right for you?

There are a lot of us – real estate brokers. The population of my State is about seven million and five hundred thousand. There are approximately thirty thousand real estate brokers in Washington State. That means that there is a real estate broker for roughly every seventy people in our State. Most of us market ourselves aggressively – so you will find us just about everywhere.

Identifying and then hiring a broker that is just right for you is more a matter of eliminating the ones that are not right for you.

As soon as you tell your five friends that you are thinking about buying a home, you are likely to get five recommendations. When your five friends tell their five friends that you are thinking of buying a home, you are likely to get several more recommendations – and so on and so on … you understand where I am going with it, right?

This is indeed not an argument against using someone who is referred to you by one of your friends or colleagues. Almost all of my business comes to me that way. I am suggesting that you *be incredibly selective* when doing so.

After months of planning and organizing and house hunting, when you finally settle on a home, you want someone in your corner who will help you acquire that home at a price that will make sense and will ensure that the entire process goes smoothly and with minimum disruption.

Start by making a list of potential hires for the job of *your* real estate broker. You will find a list of the mandated requirement of the position on page 67 of this book. You can add your wish list to that one.

As for me, regardless of how my clients find me, I put my future clients through this process that I am describing. *I discuss the mandated list with them and ask them to add their wish list.*

To find a broker that is just right for you, take all the recommendations you have got, get names from online sources and compile a list of potential hires. Then shortlist it down to five names and interview them in person – preferably on the same day.

When you start house hunting with your broker, it will be like having a new best friend for a limited engagement. You will spend a great deal of time together. You will also have to rely on the information that your broker gives you about each home. It is your broker that will present your offer to the listing broker and then negotiate with them on your behalf. Be mindful of all this as you read the following recommendations.

During my training sessions with real estate brokers and mortgage lenders, I discuss how consumers have an intuitive understanding when they are *being sold*. Most people can usually tell the difference between a professional and a snake oil salesman. I say it becuase believe that to be true. When potential clients who are considering hiring me, interview me, I invite them to use that intuition and make their judgment. I recommend that you do the same. Be methodical. Go through the process and then trust your judgment. The process isn't complicated and I am spelling it out for you next.

The broker you choose must meet your requirements in the following eight areas — and you must test each of these when you interview those who make it into your short list.

This may appear to be a lot of work. However, the fact is, you are about to undertake a substantial financial and lifestyle responsibility. The more effort you put into this phase, easier and more rewarding your home search will be.

- ♦ First and foremost you want a broker who will make you her top priority. You must always deal directly with the broker – not their team members or assistants. If she is too busy for you, she's not right for you. Teams and assistants are there to support the broker. The broker is there to serve you – be very clear about that.
- ♦ Personality matters, and in a huge way. The presence of mind and observation skills are as critical as is the ability to listen and respond accordingly. The clarity and focus of the questions they ask you will expose their mindset, commitment, efficiency, and their overall performance. Pay close attention to all that.

- Interaction with other people, responsiveness to questions and requests, trustworthiness, honesty, passion and conviction are essential traits.
- Chemistry is vital. You must feel at ease and sync with that person. Rely on your gut feeling and ascertain that you feel entirely comfortable when interacting with this person. Any awkwardness or undue pressure felt is a clear indication that the person is not the right fit.
- Empty talk full of flattery and fluffy comments isn't recommended. Pick someone who is realistic, practical, makes sound arguments and is not reluctant to point the negative aspect of things. He must use real data in his answers and explanations of his recommendations. Choose someone who will speak up and warn you if you are leaning toward making a wrong decision.
- Buying a home is an exacting task. You will be making complex decisions against deadlines, which can sometimes affect your mood and your psyche, giving way to stress. Your broker must be adept at easing the stress by staying

calm himself and assist you in working through those challenging moments.

- ♦ Ask pointed questions of all potential hires, especially about their knowledge base, skill, and comfort level with technology. Knowledge of the neighborhoods that are on your short list is another item to establish at this stage.
- ♦ After narrowing down your short list to two or three names, ask for referrals. Ask for at least three names and contact information of their clients for whom they worked within the last fifteen months. Then call and speak to each one of those people and ask them about how they feel about the person you are about to hire.

Important tip #2:

Sellers pay commission for the broker who lists their home and also for the broker who sells their home. The broker who lists the home is legally obligated to represent *only* the seller's best interest.

There is no logical reason for you to not hire a competent broker who will be legally obligated to protect and serve your interest, even though the seller would pay her.

Would you ever go to court and ask the opponent's lawyer to look after your interest?

CHAPTER FIVE

OFFER TO MUTUAL ACCEPTANCE

Act decisively when you identify a home for sale that meets your needs and desires.
Nadir Zulqernain

You obtained financing for your home acquisition, researched the neighborhoods and have settled on where you want to live. You have also developed a deeper understanding of how things work in the real estate industry. You interviewed at least five brokers, asked each of them some tough and essential questions, called their referrals and have settled on one that you concluded would best serve your needs. You have been methodical and have made an informed decision. You have accomplished all the preparatory work; it is time to act. During this phase, you must refrain from second-guessing yourself and your broker – listen to him and heed his advice. You are well equipped to make informed decisions in your best interest.

This chapter gets into the nuts and bolts of the most significant phase of the home buying process. At this stage you start viewing various homes, choose the one you like, evaluate it and make an offer to purchase it. Now, let's go further and discuss what happens when you make the offer, when it's accepted, and what to expect after you and the seller have agreed upon all terms – also known as *being under contract.*

Pull out the list of essentials and desirables you made and create a spreadsheet on Excel or Google sheet. Some of my clients have chosen to convert the numbers into colors; make an index of five colors and coded the spreadsheet with colors instead of using a number, as we discussed in chapter three. Those spreadsheets look pretty cool, are easy to use and come in handy.

Important tip #3:

Limit how many homes you see in one day. I recommend no more than four – preferably only three. When you see too many homes on the same day, they all tend to merge in your memory and cause confusion. Then, you go back to see it again and get more confused because that is not how you remembered a particular house. Spare yourself that aggravation by seeing less than four houses a day.

Available homes are at your fingertips

Most people find it very exciting in the beginning to run around and look at different homes every day and every weekend. But it can become tiresome pretty quickly.

Your broker would have set up an MLS Search for the area where you wish to purchase your new home. There are numerous options for *how to search* in MLS. You can search by:

- Large areas like cities.
- Zip codes.
- In a circle of specified distance from an address.
- In a specific school district
- In a shape of any kind, drawn on a map.

You can also choose to receive these new listing every morning, every evening or as soon as they come on the market. If you decide to use the [App I recommended](#) earlier in this book, you could check it as often as you like.

New listings come on the market every day. Wednesday and Thursday of each week see the biggest influx of new listings. To minimize the disruption to your day-to-day activities, consider receiving emails with new listings in the evening only.

Review and research those listings and send your comments to your broker. If you use the App, you can send those comments from right there. Otherwise, you can email your broker. If you use the Google sheets, you can add the homes that interest you, give your numbers or color code, add your comments, text your broker and you are all set.

Whichever method you choose to use, it is essential that you frequently communicate your thoughts to your broker. A competent broker will identify the homes in which you may have shown a keen interest and keep tabs on those properties so that she can keep you fully informed. Clear and frequent communication between you and your broker is crucial.

Minimize your legwork

Utilize the available technology to facilitate this phase for you. You can gather a great deal of data about the listings before you decide that you want to see them in person. Here are some basic things you can do to accomplish that.

- ◆ Google search the property address and look at its Street view on Google maps.
- ◆ Research that particular neighborhood to better understand its various demographics such as crime rate etc., on one of the websites that provide that information.
- ◆ If the community has a name, Google that.
- ◆ Most communities have Facebook pages these days. Look for one. These are usually filled with great information.
- ◆ Check the transportation sites to see the best way to commute from there.
- ◆ Check distances to the schools, hospitals and shopping areas.

To streamline things even further, add these columns to your Google sheet that we have discussed earlier in this book, and enter the results of your research in their respective columns. This step not only optimizes your own research, it also makes it easier for you to shares critical information with your broker. The more she understands your perspective, the better she will be able to serve you.

When you start looking at houses after following this system, you will have a lot more information at hand, which will enable you to make informed and intelligent decisions.

How long it might take to find the home that is just right for you is unpredictable. But by doing things the way I have outlined in this book, you will undoubtedly shorten that period. You will also be able to act decisively and take the right steps to acquire the right home.

Prudent homebuyers are patient; they do their research and wait to find the right home. When they see it, they act decisively.

The Paperwork

Get ready to drown in a mound of paperwork. If you have followed all the steps outlined in this book, you are well prepared, organized and have come to know your stuff – you have become an insider. You will be able to breeze through this phase.

There is no getting around the fact selling or buying a home involves a lot of paperwork. It starts with an *offer to purchase*. Only the standard forms that have been prepared, reviewed and scrutinized by lawyers are used. This serves to standardize real estate transactions and helps avoid legal issues. These forms are approved by the local MLS.

When listing a property or preparing an offer for one, brokers can only fill in the forms mentioned above. The information is filled out but no modification or alterations are permitted. On infrequent occasions when a buyer or seller insists on adding a clause, they can do so only through their real estate lawyers, and at their own expense – which can be costly.

Important tip #4:

Ask your broker to give you a complete set of blank forms that she will be using for your intended transaction, earlier on in the process. Review these forms carefully and become familiar with them. Ask your broker questions about anything that you don't fully understand. Ask her also to discuss *the sellers' disclosure* with you.

Home sellers are legally obliged to disclose all defects that they know about. When a house is listed, the owner must fill out and file a document called *the seller's disclosure*, also known as Form 17.

Things move very fast when you make an offer, and you may need to act quickly and respond promptly. There will be no time to understand what is in those forms – get to know those forms before you make an offer.

A glimpse into the listing process

Better understanding the process through which a house comes on the market can be very helpful. This information can give you clues to ask the right questions. You will also know what information you are entitled to, and what can you expect your broker to do. You will also be better prepared to make critical strategic decisions during the *offer phase*.

The broker who represents the seller is called the *listing broker*. Your broker, the one representing the *buyer* is known as the *selling broker*. The listing broker researches the market place, evaluates the condition of the house and suggests a listing price to the seller. The seller makes the final decision about the price at which the house would be offered for sale to the public.

At this initial stage, the seller and the listing broker also come to an agreement with regards to the *commission* would be paid to the Firm that employs the listing broker. It is either a fixed amount or a percentage of the final sale price. This is done in writing, using a *listing agreement*.

As a side note, reread Important Tip #2.

There is no way for your broker or you to be certain about how thorough the seller's initial market research was, how realistic is the listing price, and what factors may have impacted the pricing decision. The listing broker is duty bound to not disclose that information, even if she knew that.

Your research and the local expertise of your broker will be the determining factor here. You will need to decide what price makes sense to you, and then proceed accordingly.

Pre-listing inspection by seller

It can be a brilliant move by a savvy home seller to have his house inspected by a licensed house inspector, prior to listing it for sale. Then take the list of the deficiencies that the inspector would have produced and get each item fixed; and make available that inspection report and documentation of the work completed, to all potential buyers.

Home sellers who take this vital step give themselves an edge and protect themselves from unexpected and unpleasant surprises. It also scuttles buyer's attempt to renegotiate the price after conducting their house inspection. Disclosing all the deficiencies and the repairs done to fix those makes it easier for the buyer to move forward.

In chapter four I identified the responsibilities and obligations every broker owes to her client. The *listing broker* for the house you are interested in is legally obligated and owes those duties to his client, *the seller*, not to a potential buyer.

Making the offer

Crafting and then submitting an *offer* to purchase a house commences the legal interaction between a seller and a buyer. Most often things move quickly after your broker submits your offer to the listing broker; who in turn must present it to his client right away.

Offers specify an expiration date and expire at 9 pm on that date. For strategic reasons, prudent buyers give the seller only a few hours to respond.

Specific contract arrangements can be verbal but the law requires that real estate contracts must be in writing. Verbal communication is not binding in this case. The seller also must respond in writing before the deadline or your offer would expire.

Upon receiving an offer, a seller has three options to respond. She can accept it, make a *counteroffer* or merely ignore it — the response to your offer, whether *acceptance* or counteroffer is also required to be in writing. Even the slightest modification in your original offer makes it a counteroffer.

The act of making a counteroffer by the seller terminates the initial offer made by the buyer and starts a new contract; now being offered by the seller to the buyer. The buyer has the same three options to respond, as described above for the seller.

When representing a buyer, I like to craft our offer in such a way that the seller counters it back to us, preferably only with minor modifications. I make every effort to keep my clients in control and have the final say. It is always the best position to be when engaged in negotiations.

How much to offer

Offering a significantly lower amount than the listing price, without valid reasons, is usually not the best way to start the negotiations. Be realistic and reasonable. You and your broker have researched the house, and your broker would have given you an estimate as to its value. Unless it is a desperate sale, stay close to the estimated value.

As described earlier in this book, the amount of earnest money included with the offer and the strength of your pre-approval letter from your lender will be the two significant factors that will determine the strength of your offer.

In competitive markets where good homes are in short supply, non-monetary considerations can play a part as well. These would include the length of time before closing, occupancy dates and softening or removing of certain contingencies by the buyer.

How much you offer, how hard you negotiate, and how much ground you give in – depends on how much you want that house and how other homes in that specific market have been selling.

Be rational and logical. You are making a lifestyle and more importantly, a significant financial decision. The numbers must make sense.

You must also consider your options if you chose not to acquire that specific house. How would it impact your life? What are the possibilities of you finding another home in the same neighborhood – and other similar factors? These decisions tend to be difficult and only buyers can make those.

Contingencies

Real estate contracts are carefully written to facilitate real estate transaction and protect all sides involved. It is my view that these contracts can provide the buyers with a slight edge when they utilize the contingencies fittingly. Of course, the underlying *Caveat Emptor* principal always applies.

After the buyer and the seller agree on all the terms, and *the offer* becomes *mutually accepted*, various parties have yet to take several crucial steps.

- The buyer still has to carry out inspections.
- The lender has to rerun the loan numbers based on the purchase price and obtain an appraisal.
- The title company must complete its due diligence and verify the ownership of the house.

The offer document anticipates all this and allocates specific timeframes within which the buyer must complete these activities. The buyer's right to withdraw from the agreement if the result of any of these activities turns out to be unsatisfactory is called a *contingency*. As a buyer, you will also have the option to remove a particular contingency regardless if it has been satisfied or not. Often in robust seller's markets, this aspect becomes part of negotiations.

It is my considered opinion that a buyer must never bargain away any of the contingencies that were written in the agreement for their protection.

As outlined above, three main contingencies are built into the contract to purchase.

First is **the inspection contingency**. As a buyer, you are permitted to refuse to proceed if a licensed home inspector found *deficiencies* that you, in your sole judgment consider *worrisome*. You are not obligated to provide any justification for your decision. Often, an agreement is reached between the two parties about how to address those issues. It is to be noted that the buyer is in full control at this point.

Although not required by law, you must always get the house inspected, even if it is a brand new house. When all of the issues that surfaced during the inspection have been resolved, you can sign off on the *inspection contingency*.

The financing contingency enables a buyer to break that contract if their mortgage loan application is rejected due to reasons beyond their control. Typically, this contingency is not removed till the very end.

Lastly, ***the appraisal contingency*** goes hand-in-hand with the financing contingency. Your lender orders the appraisal and an in independent, licensed appraiser performs it. The appraised value forms the basis of your mortgage loan, right alongside your creditworthiness. Previously agreed upon loan terms can change significantly if the appraised value is less than the purchase price.

There can be other contingencies. Even a relatively new broker will be able to help you identify those.

Important tip #5:

Even after you sign off on the appraisal contingency, you must not remove the financing contingency. These two are closely tied together – however, other issues could spell trouble for your loan approval, later in the process.

CHAPTER SIX

FROM ACCEPTANCE TO CLOSE

Our value proposition is accuracy and convenience.

Ben Caballero

Your offer was accepted, and you are now under contract. When this happens, the MLS status of that property will reflect as *Pending Inspection*. Your broker would have specified the number of days within which you are required to complete an inspection of the house that you have agreed to purchase.

Be mindful that if you fail to have the property inspected within the specified period, the inspection contingency will be automatically waived.

It is entirely possible that the house inspector you hire might identify issues in his inspection report that would require a specialist. For example, if there are concerns about the electric wiring or furnace or termites – these types of things will need inspectors who are qualified and licensed in those areas to inspect and give you their reports.

Two crucial points are to be noted.

1. It is the buyer's obligation to pay for each of these inspections.
2. The inspection addendum to the purchase and sale agreement would have specified how long the buyer would be allowed to complete these supplementary inspections.

Upon completing the inspection(s), you, as a buyer would have three options.

1) Accept the inspection report as is.
2) Reject the inspection and through your broker inform the seller that you are withdrawing your *offer to purchase.*
3) You can demand that the seller could repair or replace some or all of the items that the inspection has identified as problematic – or the

seller could compensate you financially for those deficiencies.

Unless there are serious structural or other significant problems with the property, most folks opt for the third option mentioned above.

The negotiations in this phase can be grueling, and not always pleasant. It is at this stage that the value of having a seasoned and competent broker in your corner becomes clearer.

Your broker must be a good negotiator. More importantly, he must understand the nuances and the rules that govern this phase. This is the phase when an inept broker could cost her clients thousands of dollars, and an exceptional one could save you thousands of dollars.

Whilst you are dealing with the inspection, several other duly licensed and bonded professionals, most of whom you may never meet face to face, will go to work and perform numerous critical functions. Your broker is responsible for staying on top of these processes – all you need to do is to ensure that you check in with your broker frequently and get sufficient and relevant updates.

Instead of wondering as to who are all these people, you can take comfort in knowing that they have your best interests at heart.

In the following pages I will give you an overview of each entity, individual and of their functions.

House Inspection

Although legally not required, almost everyone who buys a home gets a home inspection done. Even when a buyer may have been pushed into waiving the inspection contingency in a multi-offer, extremely competitive market, a competent broker would have waived only the *right to renegotiate the price* after the inspection and not the right to the inspection itself.

Full house-inspections are thorough and detailed. The inspector follows a systematic approach to cover numerous systems within the house and its immediate surroundings. You must pay close attention to these *hot spots* issues.

- ♦ **Mildew and mold** – presence of odors and visible stains caused by mildew and mold are a grave matter. Mildew odors are a strong indication that the basement if there is one, or crawl space or even the attic is likely to have a high level of moisture. It is almost impossible to remove mildew; the process of removing mold is exceptionally costly.

Only two issues mandate a recommendation of withdrawing the offer, when I come across them. In addition to the one I just mentioned, the other one is leakage or seepage of water.

- **Damp basements, crawlspaces or attic** – the home inspector will carefully inspect the walls and floors for patches of mildew and signs of dampness – and will use a meter to measure the amount of moisture present in that space. Excessive moisture in a home is a serious issue because it causes the building materials to deteriorate and it also attracts insects.

- **Foundation inspection** – while essential, it can be tricky to carry out. You must insist that your inspector take a look at the foundation. If he finds something that doesn't look right, he'll likely recommend bringing in a structural engineer. You will then have to decide how to proceed from there.

- **Roof and chimney** – the condition of shingles or other roof covering will be good indications of the state of the roof, along with an interior inspection of lines just beneath the ceiling. In some States, a licensed roof inspector is required to inspect the roof.

- **Plumbing** problems – your home inspector will check the water pressure in the house by turning on multiple faucets, running the dishwasher and flushing all the toilets, all at the same time. You can expect your home inspector to check the septic system as well if the house has one.
- **Electrical systems** – the house inspector will check the electrical panel and circuit breaker configuration to make sure that it is adequate for the needs of that particular house and that work was according to the *code* at the time.
- **In addition** – to the items mentioned above, your home inspector will check the heating and cooling systems to ensure that they are in good working condition.

Your home inspector will provide you a written, detailed and thorough report with photographs of deficiencies and his recommendations on how to resolve the various issues he would identify in that report.

As a buyer, you pay for this inspection report and it is yours to keep. Let your broker help you figure out the most strategic way to obtain the most favorable response from the seller.

These negotiations can become very complicated. Ask your broker if she is fully aware of the nuances of rules that govern this part of a transaction – if she is not, ask her to consult with her managing broker.

The Appraisal

In chapter two I discussed how a lender determines the viability of your mortgage loan application, as it relates to you, as a borrower. That aspect has to do with your ability to repay the loan. An appraisal deals with the second critical element of a mortgage loan – the collateral. The lender must independently establish a fair market value of the collateral that will secure your mortgage loan; the property you have chosen to acquire. The lender must do so through a third party, in this case, a licensed appraiser.

The primary function of an appraiser is to establish the *fair market value* of a property at any given time. The *Fair Market Value* is the price that *a knowledgeable, willing, and free of duress buyer is likely to pay to a prepared, knowledgeable, and free of duress seller of real property*. The transaction must be at arms-length. The price you have offered to pay will factor into the appraiser's calculations along with numerous other factors.

Appraisers are independent, licensed professionals who are expected to be completely unbiased and driven only by data. They also have specific guidelines that they must follow to gather that data. Neither the seller nor that buyer can have any direct contact with the appraisal company that your lender will hire.

The independence of the appraiser is crucial. It is considered to be so important that even the lenders are not permitted to communicate directly with the appraisers. Appraisal management companies employ qualified and licensed appraisers. The lender sends their request to the company, which, through an internal process, allocates an appraiser for that work. The buyer bears the cost of an appraisal.

If you have been diligent in your initial evaluation process and your broker has advised you well, it is highly likely that the prices you have agreed to pay will be consistent with the market conditions. It doesn't matter if the appraised value turns out to be higher than the mutually agreed upon sales price.

Appraisers base most of their calculations on recent sales of similar properties within a specified area. They follow a specific mathematical formula to adjust the prices due to variants in different properties. They allocate land values; adjust for the physical condition of the property, consider its additional features and the neighborhood itself.

A professionally done appraisal is an all-encompassing home valuation. Most of the time, it is completely accurate. Occasionally, there can be a difference of opinion.

Lenders base their loan calculations on the purchase prices specified in the agreement or the appraised price *whichever is less*.

If the *appraised value* turns out to be significantly lower than the agreed upon price, then you must take a deep breath and reconsider things carefully. Identify the key issues and then make a knowledgeable decision.

A lower appraisal tends to reopen the negotiations between the seller and the buyer. This is another occasion when the depth of knowledge, negotiations skills and understanding of the nuances of this phase by your broker can play a pivotal role. You will have three options.

- ♦ Use your appraisal contingency and reject the appraisal; withdraw from the offer.

- ◆ Renegotiate a lower price with the seller to reflect the lower appraised value
- ◆ Pay for the difference yourself. Remember, you will need to pay for the entire amount in deficit in cash. Lenders do not lend any portion of that.

For example, if the mutually agreed upon purchase price is $600,000 and your down payment was to be ten percent; your mortgage loan amount would have been $540,000. You would have based your financial consideration on these numbers. If the appraised value turns out to be $570,000, you will need to come up with an extra $27,000 in real cash. This would throw off your financial calculation. You'll also need strong reasons to pay a 5% premium for that property.

Title

The *title* is the document that establishes a legal claim to the ownership of a specific real property to the person named therein.

The seller is required to deliver that document to the *closing agent* at the time of, or before *closing*. The title itself does not identify any encumbrances against the property. Those records are at the county's office.

People often use real property as collateral for loans. Additionally, there can be other types of claims that can encumber a property. There is also the question of accuracy of the boundaries of the real estate.

How land and home ownership records are registered and recorded can be a complicated discussion; one that is beyond the scope of this book's subject.

Before a listing broker lists a house on MLS, she obtains a *preliminary title report* and includes it in the listing. This document contains only the information currently recorded in public records for that property. The title company does not research any of that information for authenticity at this early stage.

Title insurance offers protection to buyers, sellers, and lenders against encumbrances and other issues that may arise regarding the accuracy of the information contained in the title report. Almost all different types of insurance policies cover potential losses against events that might happen in the future. Title insurance policies protect against events that may already have occurred – and may have resulted in claims against that particular real property – and were either unreported or unclaimed.

The seller purchases the *sellers' policy*, also called the *owner's policy*. This policy protects the buyer by assuring that the seller's title of the property is vested appropriately, and is free from encumbrances except those identified in the title report. Those items are called *exceptions* in the policy and are excluded from coverage of the new policy.

The seller's policy also covers any potential damages that the buyer may suffer if the title turns out to be defective, or unmarketable. Usually, the purchase price of the home is the amount of liability covered in the seller's title insurance policy.

The buyer purchases the lender's title insurance policy, which does not provide any coverage to the buyer – it protects the lender against items identified in the preceding paragraph, to the extent of the loan amount.

As is the case with most insurance policies, the documents for *title insurance* are lengthy and complex. The policies come with options to add items at additional costs. The most common type of policy is called *standard coverage* and suffices in most cases.

You need not go shopping around for a better policy. The closing agent will initiate an application when she opens escrow and handle this aspect for you. The cost of this policy will be included in your closing costs.

The escrow, the closing agent and closing

Professionals from five connected but different fields participate in a real estate transaction. Each field has its unique set of rules and guidelines that these professionals must follow. Some of these rules and guidelines may occasionally overlap and even conflict with each other.

Your real estate broker is expected to be aware of most of these rules and stays engaged on each front to ensure that your interests are protected.

Once again, I want to refresh your memory about the underlying principle of *Caveat Emptor* as it relates to real estate transactions. *It remains your responsibility to protect yourself.*

This section of the current chapter may be tedious to read because it contains dry and dull information. We are now getting into the legalities, technicalities and the documentation involved.

Read it a few times if you need to. Make sure you understand various points and be mindful of the information herein. I recommend that you use this chapter as a reference guide when you get to this final phase to help you in being diligent and to safeguard your interests

I also recommend that you do a final walk through the day before you are scheduled to sign the papers and confirm that the property is in the condition that you expect it to be – if any concerns develop at this stage, your broker and the listing broker will work together to find a satisfactory resolution.

The *purchase and sale agreement* protects you by having a clause that puts the burden on the seller to ensure that the property is in the same condition when you saw it initially.

We have discussed the real estate side in detail and touched upon the lending process. You also went through the inspection process. You have reviewed the preliminary and full title report. At this final stage the money will exchange hands, a great deal of paperwork will be completed and you will become the legal owner of your new home.

This final phase has always been intriguing to me. Most homebuyers do not make the effort to fully understand much of what goes on at this stage. They are exhausted from house hunting, negotiating and then getting into inspection issues. They tend to go along with whatever their real estate broker or their lender tells them. That is not the best approach.

Important tip #6

When you get to this phase, *make diligence the central theme*. Be mindful of every step that you take. Ask questions, double check the information.

Put your broker to task and have her get you the answers that you need. You are about to hand over a chunk of money and take on a significant financial liability. Any errors or omissions by you at this stage will be financially burdensome. You must not take this phase lightly.

Your real estate broker has no active part at this stage. However, he remains your source of information and should be ready to assist you in any way. Most real estate brokers either attend the closing with you or are available by phone, in case you wish to discuss any aspect of the closing documents that you are signing.

What does this mean?

Here are a few definitions to help you better understand the meaning of these terms – it is right about at this stage when people start throwing these jargons at you.

The Escrow is legally defined as a bond, deed, or other document kept in the custody of a third party and it takes effect only when previously specified conditions have been fulfilled.

Escrow instructions are defined as the written instructions given by a buyer and a seller, engaged in a specific real estate transaction, to the closing agent identified in the purchase and sale agreement. The closing agent prepares these instructions and obtains approval from both, the seller and the buyer.

The closing agent is a licensed, bonded person who usually works for a large company, and handles this final phase. Most title companies provide closing or escrow services in addition to providing title insurance. In some states, the law requires that you hire a lawyer to do the closing.

Closing is the consummation of the transaction when various conditions have been met, and the legal documents are signed, notarized and recorded.

Important tip #7

Don't just peruse through the escrow instructions and sign the document. You must review it carefully and ensure that it is consistent with the purchase and sale agreement that you signed.

This is especially important because in case of a dispute, the closing agent will follow the escrow instructions and not the purchase and sale agreement.

Specified conditions, as referenced in the *definition of escrow*, these fall into four main categories as it relates to a real estate transaction.

The seller must provide a marketable title that is free of any encumbrances that were not documented in the *comprehensive title report*.

The title company must provide a detailed title report that also includes confirmation that the property is free of any encumbrances and any other legal obligations that may not have been previously identified.

The lender must be satisfied with the information it received; must have completed its *processing and underwriting* of the loan and be ready to advance the funds.

***The buyer*:**

    a) Must be ready to deposit the *funds needed to close* with the closing agent,

    b) Must be satisfied with all of the information in the title report and other documents,

c) Must have accepted the loan terms offered by the lender,

d) Must have received the loan documents within the legally required deadline,

e) Must have reviewed and approved those loan documents.

The closing agent is responsible for carrying out the escrow instructions which are based on the purchase and sale agreement that both of the parties signed. Additionally, the closing agent interacts with the lender and ensures that the lender's requirements are satisfied, so the mortgage loan funds can become available at or before closing.

The closing agent and the process of escrow protect buyers, sellers, and lenders because as a neutral third party, it ensures that all required conditions have been met before handing over any cash to the seller or the keys to the buyer.

The closing agent's functions:

1) Receive the funds – from the buyer and the lender.
2) Receive the ownership deed from the seller and ensure that it is a marketable title.
3) Review the loan documents and ensure that the loan terms match with the escrow instructions. The lender is responsible for the accuracy of the loan documents.
4) Prepare a closing statement in cooperation with the lender and make it available to the seller and buyer before the signing of the documents. The lender is obligated to provide the borrower a closing disclosure that spells out the loan terms, costs and any other fees. The lender is also bound to give the borrower three days to review this document. The closing statement is primarily based on this disclosure.
5) Have the seller and buyer sign their respective documents.
6) Pay off all of the existing liabilities against the property, consistent with the purchase and sale agreement. If a certain liability cannot be paid

off right away, for example a utilities bill, the closing agent will hold that amount in escrow and pay it off later.

7) Disburse the funds to the seller.
8) Record the new deed in the new buyer's name in the county records, give the recording numbers to the brokers.

Documents to be signed by the buyer

As a buyer, you will sign the following documents at the *closing*, with the closing agent. You can request these documents be provided to you ahead of time. You will receive a copy of each after you have signed.

The loan estimate has vital information about your loan; i.e., terms, interest rate, and closing costs.

The closing disclosure spells out details of your mortgage loan. The mortgage lender is required to give you this document at least three days before closing. The loan cannot be advanced unless you have had this time to review this document.

The initial escrow statement deals with the escrow account that the lender keeps, from which your taxes and insurances are paid on your behalf.

The mortgage note is the document that legally binds you to repay the mortgage. It shows the amount and terms of the loan and spells out the lender's rights if you do not make the payments.

You assign the **deed of trust** as *collateral* for the mortgage note to formalize the lender's claim against the house for which they have lent you the funds.

After the seller and the buyer have signed the requisite documents and the closing agent has reconciled and verified all of the information, she will distribute the funds as specified in the escrow instructions. Then she will prepare the recording documents, and the company's agent will physically go to the county's recording office and register the new deed that will show you as the rightful owner of that house.

The recording office does not issue the new deed on the spot. The deed is prepared later and mailed to your address several weeks later. They issue *recording numbers*. The closing agent releases these numbers to both the brokers involved. When this happens, the listing broker hands off the key to the house to your broker, who will, in turn, present them to you. At this stage, you become the legal owner of the home and have its possession.

Important tip #8

This is warning that we send to all our clients. You will be well served by taking it seriously.

URGENT: WIRE FRAUD ALERT

BUYING OR SELLING?

ALWAYS CALL BEFORE YOU WIRE FUNDS!

Real estate buyers and sellers are targets for wire fraud and many have lost hundreds of thousands of dollars because they failed to take two simple steps:

1. Obtaining the phone number of your real estate broker and your escrow agent at your first meeting;
2. Calling the known phone number to speak directly with your broker or escrow officer to confirm wire instructions **PRIOR** to wiring.

BEWARE OF THE FOLLOWING SCAM:

1. An email account is hacked (this could be broker's, escrow's, or consumer's email).
2. Hacker monitors the account, waiting for the

time when consumer must wire funds. Broker, escrow, and consumer don't know that they are being monitored.

3. Hacker, impersonating broker or escrow, instructs consumer to wire funds immediately. The wire instructions are for an account controlled by the hacker. These instructions often create a sense of urgency and often explain that the broker or escrow officer cannot be reached by phone so any follow-up must be by email. When a consumer replies to this email, the email is diverted to hacker.
4. Consumer wires the funds, which are stolen by hacker with no recourse for consumer.

IMPORTANT

Never wire funds without first calling the known phone number for broker, the escrow company or the closing agent and confirming the wire instructions. DO NOT rely upon e-mail communications.

CHAPTER SEVEN

IN CONCLUSION

Plan your purchase and work your plan!
Nadir Zulqernain

My nine-point home acquisition system is sprinkled throughout the previous chapters. Following this system will give you the information you need to go through the process of home acquisition confidently, while staying in control at every stage.

This approach will also make your home buying experience smooth and hassle-free and protect you against inadvertent mistakes that can often be very costly.

Here is a point-by-point summary of the nine-point home buying system that we have discussed.

1. Figure out your finances and obtain an underwriters loan approval *before* you start searching for your new home. Limit the purchase price of your home to no more than ninety percent of your affordability amount.
2. Make a list of your *essentials* and *desirables* – what you must have and what will be a luxury to have. Identify which ones you can live without.
3. Choose your neighborhood as carefully as your home. Thoroughly research all relevant aspects.
4. Hire a highly competent real estate professional through a careful selection process. Hire the one who will take the time to understand your needs and competently represent your interests.
5. Carefully plan out all aspects of your major financial purchase and then stick to your plan.
6. Utilize all of the search tools that you can find, to locate your home. Cross-reference your information from one source with other sources.
7. Fully understand every aspect of an offer to purchase before you submit that offer – your real estate broker is responsible for helping you accomplish that. Always get a home inspection and still do a walk-through the before closing.

8. Handle your money with care and write checks only to those who are authorized to receive it. It is your money. Guard it carefully.
9. Ask questions. Ask more questions; of your broker, your lender, your home inspector, your escrow closer. Make sure you fully understand the answers that you get.

In my real estate practice, a wealth of experience gained over the last two decades enables me to guide and proffer feasible solutions to my client's diverse real estate needs and enables me to ensure a streamlined selling and buying experience for them.

My team members and I use a seven-point system to accomplish what I have outlined in the preceding paragraphs. This information will help you hire the right broker.

We:

1) Commit to represent our client diligently and to safeguard their interests during every phase.
2) Ensure that we keep our clients fully informed at every step of the way.

3) Use leading-edge skills and the best tools available for our business to gain every advantage for our clients.

4) Provide our clients with leading-edge research and data that we gather using advanced technologies.

5) Craft offers that while being highly desirable by the sellers; also gain our clients every possible advantage. This phase is about knowing the rules and understanding the nuances – we excel at that, and have negotiations skills are second to none.

6) Assist and advise our clients in dealing with the house inspection, title and escrow matters, and all other pre-closing steps.

7) Support and assist with any other issues that might (and they often do) surface at any stage. We are committed to serving our clients to the best of our abilities.

Buying your home with confidence

TOPIC INDEX

1. Chapter One: Home buying basics. Page 16
    a. Navigate three separate paths. Page 18
    b. Altering a house purchase is costly. Page 20
2. Chapter Two: Money Matters – Page 23
    a. Document the source of your income. Page 25
    b. Track record of repaying debts. Page 27
    c. Credit score impact. Page 28
    d. Pre-Approval and pre-qualification. Page 31
    e. The Ernest Money and Down Payment. Page 36
    f. Down Payment Funds. Page 39
    g. Proof of funds. Page 40
    h. Sourcing and seasoning of funds. Page 41
    i. Gift funds. Page 42
3. Chapter Three: Finding your ideal home. Page 43
    a. Important tip #1. Page 44
    b. Make the list. Page 45
    c. Select your neighborhood. Page 48
    d. Start your search. Page 50
    e. What is an MLS and how does it work? Page 53

f. The most effective way to search. Page 56
4. Chapter Four: Find the perfect one. Page 59
   a. How is the industry structured? Page 61
   b. How does real estate licensing work? Page 65
   c. Responsibilities of a broker. Page 67
   d. How to recognize a good broker? Page 70
   e. Essential requirements of a broker. Page 73
   f. Important tip #2. Page 79
5. Chapter Five: From Offer to Mutual. Page 80
   a. Important tip #3. Page 82
   b. Available homes at your fingertips. Page 83
   c. Minimize your legwork. Page 85
   d. The paperwork. Page 87
   e. Important Tip #4. Page 88
   f. A glimpse into the listing process. Page 89
   g. Pre-listing inspection by sellers. Page 91
   h. Making an offer. Page 92
   i. How much to offer. Page 94
   j. Contingencies. Page 96
   k. Important tip #5. Page 99
6. Chapter Six. From acceptance to close Page 100

- a. House inspection. Page 104
- b. The appraisal. Page 108
- c. Title. Page 112
- d. The escrow, closing agent and closing. Page 115
- e. Important tip #6. Page 118
- f. What does this mean? Page 119
- g. Important tip #7. Page 121
- h. Specified Conditions. Page 122
- i. The closing agent's functions. Page 124
- j. Documents signed by the buyer. Page 126
- k. Information Tip #8. Page 128

7. Chapter Seven. Nine-point buying system. Page 130

www.ingramcontent.com/pod-product-compliance
Lightning Source LLC
Chambersburg PA
CBHW072143170526
45158CB00004BA/1485